Mastering the Ukulele for Beginners

A Step-by-Step Guide with Follow-Along Videos

By: Jake Harper

Table of Contents

Chapter 1: Introduction 1

Chapter 2: The Parts of the Ukulele 3

Chapter 3: The Relationship Between Ukulele and Guitar...........9

Chapter 4: How to Read Tabs and Chord Charts......................13

Chapter 5: Basic Chords and Progressions 21

Chapter 6: Note Names (Optional) 28

Chapter 7: Basic Rhythms and Strumming Patterns..................32

Chapter 8: Barre Chords..40

Chapter 9: Scales and Basic Music Theory (Optional) 46

Chapter 10: Different Types of 7th Chords................................54

Chapter 11: Full Chord Chart..64

Throughout this book there are musical examples, audio, and video recordings to follow along with on your journey to learn how to play your instrument.

Whenever you see the following outline:

1. Mary Had a Little Lamb (One String)

Please follow along with the recordings at the following website: https://bit.ly/3VnIvwv

Chapter 1

Introduction

Aloha and Mahalo! You've decided to pick up the ukulele! It's a beautiful instrument - one that anybody can make sing with not too much practice! As such, it's been used in the occasional cringe YouTube apology video, but don't let that deter you!

While we may associate the ukulele with twee indie bands and YouTubers, it was originally introduced to Hawaii in the 1880s, based on several different small guitars brought by Portuguese immigrants to the islands. It comes in many sizes, but you'll most likely get your hands on a "standard" or "soprano" uke. All of the *main* models come with 4 strings (although some ultra-rare models have 6 or 8 strings), and we'll talk more about those later. It's been famously used by musicians ranging from George Harrison to Billie Eilish, but was played perhaps most famously by Israel Kamakawiwoʻole. Israel, or IZ for short, was named "the voice of Hawaii" by NPR in 2010 due to his extreme success through the dulcet tones of his actual voice, as well as the ukulele. His medley covering "Somewhere Over the Rainbow/What a Wonderful World" has been featured in countless movies and TV shows, and he even used his music for good - he was a vocal activist who believed tourism in Hawaii had subjugated natives such as himself, and spoke out on this issue through his music. He is still the single most successful Hawaiian musician of all time, and as such, serves as the de facto mascot of the ukulele.

Now that you've gotten a cursory history of the instrument, let's learn about its parts and strings!

Chapter 2

The Parts of the Ukulele

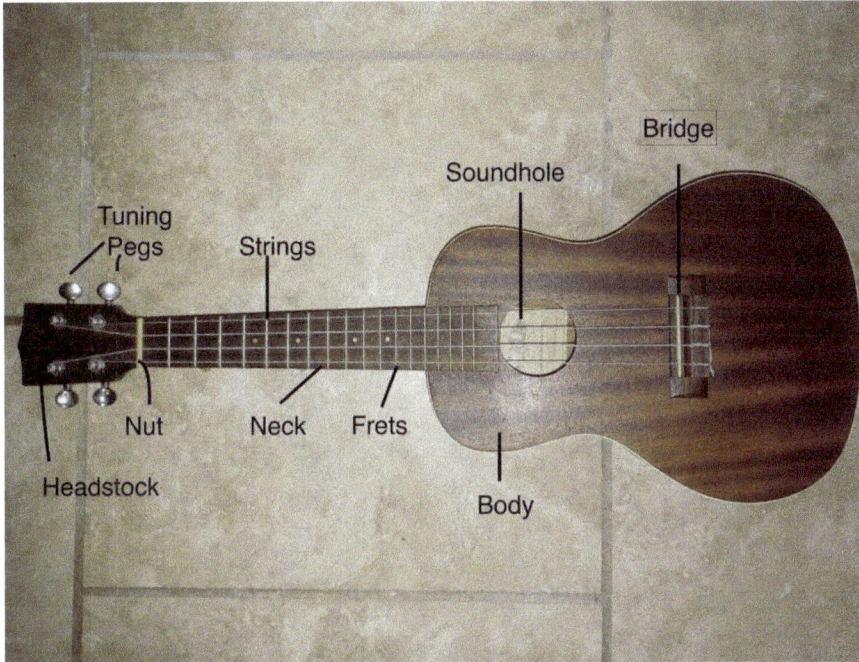

Headstock

The **headstock** sits at the top of the ukulele. It will be on your left if you play a standard, right-handed ukulele. Upon it sits the tuning pegs.

Tuning Pegs

The **tuning pegs** create the right amount of tension on the strings to make the desired pitches - or "notes." You can bring these pitches up or down by tightening or loosening these tuning pegs. This is how you can change the overall tuning of the ukulele if you want to play in an alternate tuning. **Remember** - if you want to lower a string's pitch: go too low, and then tighten it back up to the required pitch. This will keep the string's pitch (and tension) from sagging as you play. This is also a good idea when tuning drums, or any stringed instrument.

Nut

The **nut** sits atop the neck, and at the base of the headstock. As mentioned in the next definition, it acts as the first fret (but is stronger, and guides the strings toward the tuning pegs).

Frets

The **frets** help you play different notes or pitches (as well as chords - which are groups of many different notes or pitches). They are the bars - vertical in this picture - that are spread across the neck. In order to play different notes, you press a finger down on the empty neck spaces *between* the frets (on a standard right-handed ukulele, you'd typically press down on the frets with fingers on your left hand). As such, some people call these *spaces* in-between the frets, "frets." That's because it's the easiest way to describe how to play something. The first "fret" - in terms of the first "space" you can place a finger - is to the right of the nut. If a tab tells you to play a "0" on a given string, this means they want you to pluck or strum a string without pressing down anywhere on the neck. Ukulele chord charts will show a picture of the nut and the first few frets, and illustrate where you should push down on the frets and strum (most chords will use only the first few frets -

and if they want you to position your hand higher, the first fret you use will be numbered). Here are the numbers of the frets:

Some beginners find it helpful to put small sticky notes on the side of the neck closest to you with numbers for reference. Notice that additional landmarks are included on the ukulele (with the dots on the neck for the 5th, 7th, 10th, and 12th frets - some guitars and ukuleles will replace the 10th fret with the 9th, and guitars will often have a dot on the 15th fret as well).

Strings

The **strings** are what you play! As mentioned, you can change the pitches of these strings with the tuning knobs. You can plug the strings individually with any finger, or you can pleasantly strum across all of them to play chords (which is the way ukulele is more commonly played). You can even do both at the same time and play chord-melodies. They're generally made of nylon on a standard ukulele, and you play them with the fingers on your right hand (again, on a standard right-handed ukulele).

Neck

The strings run up along the neck, and the **neck** is how you actually play the different notes and chords (since you're not technically pressing on the frets, but the spaces on the neck in-between the frets). If you somehow end up with a fretless ukulele, you'd press directly on the lines (that *hopefully* are there) where the frets *would* be (which would, again, be *on* the neck). A fretless ukulele *without* those lines is only for very advanced players (which is true for any fretless instrument - even a fretless instrument with those lines is unfamiliar for anybody who isn't well-versed). You also hold the ukulele with your left hand on the neck, with the back of the neck resting in the palm of your left hand, and with your left thumb wrapping around the neck.

Body

The **body** is the center of the instrument! It's where the sound reverberates, and where you hold the ukulele with your right forearm. It's much smaller and lighter than the body of a guitar, which is why the ukulele is such a great instrument for kids! The heavy weight of some instruments can be a barrier that prevents children from excelling, but the ukulele doesn't have that problem.

Soundhole

As the sound of your playing reverberates in the body of the instrument, it then escapes out of the **soundhole**. If you were to be playing into a microphone, you'd want to point the mic at the soundhole. Your strumming fingers will get in the way of the sound traveling out, but the sound will still get picked up by the mic (as well as the ears of listeners if you are in an acoustic, or un-mic'ed situation).

Bridge

The tuning pegs would have nothing to hold onto to create the right amount of tension for pleasant sounding pitches if it weren't for the bridge. The strings are tied around the bridge, as well as the tuning pegs - and the ends attached to the bridge are stationary, so that the ends wrapped around the tuning pegs can be stretched or loosened to the appropriate pitches.

Chapter 3

The Relationship Between Ukulele and Guitar

If you already play guitar, then you probably already know this. But we'll state it here anyway: if you can already play the guitar, then you can already play the ukulele! In fact, learning the ukulele is a great way to learn the guitar.

Ukuleles come in many sizes and tunings. But, most likely, you'll end up with a standard, soprano ukulele.

Let's take a quick detour, and talk about the guitar for a second. The standard tuning for a guitar is as follows - E, A, D, G, B, E (starting from the lowest pitch string - the closest to the player - and finishing with the highest pitch string, which is the furthest from the player). The guitar is held the same way as a ukulele - the player holds the neck of the guitar with the left hand, presses down on the frets with the left and, and plucks or strums the strings with the right hand. When the player looks down at the guitar, this is the view they see:

By the way, touching on the landmark dots from earlier - there are dots on the 5th, 7th, 9th, 12th, 15th, and 17th frets on this guitar. Anyway - so, at this angle, the lowest string is an E, the second lowest is an A, etc. Each string gets higher, and the reason two strings are both an "E" is that they are in different ranges (the high E is two octaves higher). Based on how high a note is, specific pitches will be labeled by which "octave" they are (since notes repeat - they go ABCDEFGABCDEFG etc.). So the guitar strings are as follows:

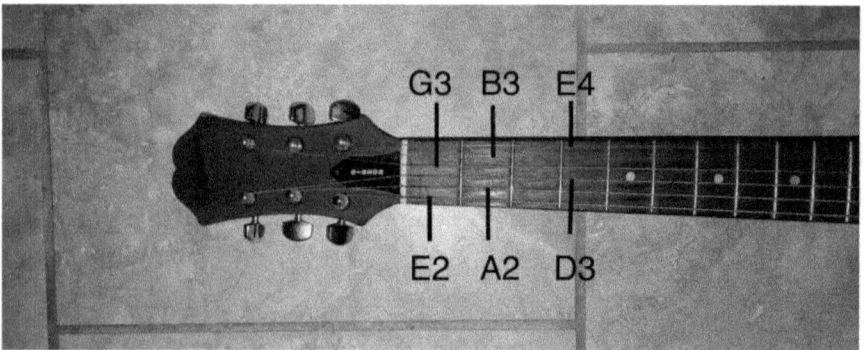

Maybe this is confusing to you. That's fine, you don't need to understand any of this. But the (musical) *distance* between the strings is what we're talking about. If you press on the 5th fret of each string, you will get the same pitch as the next string (if you press on the 5th fret of the E2 string, you will get a sound identical to the A2 string). The one exception is that if you press down on the 4th fret of the G3 string, you will get the same sound as a B3.

So the 5th string is 5 half-steps higher than the 6th string, the 4th string is 5 half-steps higher than the 5th string, the 3rd string is 5 half-steps higher than the 4th string, the 2nd string is **4** half-steps higher than the 3rd string, and the top string is 5 half-steps higher than the 2nd string. All of this can be changed with alternate tunings, but this is the standard tuning of the guitar.

WHY DID I JUST GO INTO SO MUCH DETAIL? Well, the ukulele has different notes than the guitar - of course it does, there are only four strings. But the *distances between* the notes are *identical* to that of the top four strings of a guitar - with one small change. The fourth from top string - where the D3 would be on a guitar - is one octave higher than you'd expect. So the notes for the strings on the ukulele are as follows:

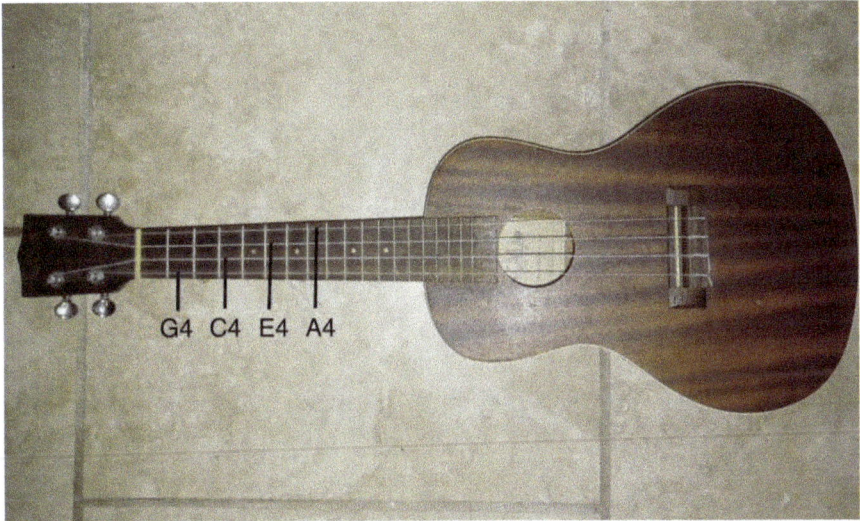

These octave numbers reset on C, so all of them are in the same octave. And, the *second* from closest string to the player is actually the lowest in pitch. The closest string (G4) is actually the second *highest* in pitch, right below the A4. Once again, maybe this is all confusing, and you just want to play some chords on the ukulele. If that's the case, that's fine, and you can ignore this whole section.

The Point is This:

If you learn *chords* on the ukulele, you will have learned chord shapes that are reusable on the guitar (although, there are two strings not accounted for if you switch to guitar). If you can already play chords the acoustic guitar, you can play them on the ukulele (although they will be transposed - a "G" shape on the guitar will get you a "C" chord on the ukulele, and a "D" shape on the guitar will get you a "G" chord on the ukulele). That G4 on the closest string will throw a slight wrench in your single-note melody plans if you're coming over from guitar, but you'll most likely be able to handle it just fine. People mostly just play chords on the ukulele anyway! Even if you use a smaller ukulele, or use the most common alternate tuning - every string will be tuned up a whole step. So it's all transposed up one whole step compared to the main tuning, just like the ukulele is transposed up from the guitar. I like to describe "transposition" as musically moving an entire house with a giant forklift (assuming that's the tool you'd use? I don't know, I'm not a construction worker). Technically everything moved, but the kitchen is still the same distance from the bathroom.

Even lower pitched ukuleles reuse the *bottom* four strings of a guitar (as do the electric and upright basses) - at least in terms of the distance between the notes. All of these stringed instruments are made to be "cross-platform" instruments, in video game terms - getting proficient at one makes learning another much easier.

So with all that said - let's play the ukulele!

Chapter 4

How to Read Tabs and Chord Charts

So once you start playing the ukulele, you'll inevitably want to look up songs to learn how to play. Don't worry, we'll still avoid real music notation and sheet music - this will work for anyone, no need to know your music theory! You may have even already seen these before, or even understand how to read them. But we'll cover them here just to be safe. Let's start with tabs.

How To Read Tabs

Tabs are great. They tell you how to play something note for note without you learning music notation. They're also great, because they work to teach you chord shapes too! Chord charts will only teach you the chord shapes, but we can show you how to use both here.

Tabs use a drawn depiction of the strings in lieu of a music staff. Instead of pitches being displayed with typical musical notes on a music staff, they're portrayed with numbers. When you see a number on the tab, do two simple things: first, push down on the fret corresponding with the number on the pictured string - then, pluck the string (with the finger of your choice)! Try to do these at the exact same time (or, err on the side of pushing down on the string with your left hand first - sometimes, it's actually good to do this well in advance of plucking the string).

These are two tabs that illustrate how to play "Mary Had a Little Lamb" in the key of C. One stays on one string, and one switches between strings (both rely on the traditional tuning I mentioned earlier).

```
A |-------------------------------------------------------------|
E |-------------------------------------------------------------| x1
C |4-2-0-2-4-4-4---2-2-2---4-7-7---4-2-0-2-4-4-4-4-2-2-4-2-0|
G |-------------------------------------------------------------|
```

🔊

1. Mary Had a Little Lamb (One String)

2. Mary Had a Little Lamb (One String - Over the Shoulder)

```
A |-------------------------------------------------------------|
E |0-------0-0-0--------0------0-------0-0-0-0-----0----| x1
C |---2-0-2---------2-2-2--------------2-0-2--------2-2---2-0|
G |-------------------------0-0--------------------------------|
```

🔊

3. Mary Had a Little Lamb (Three String)

4. Mary Had a Little Lamb (Three String - Over the Shoulder)

Again, each line represents a string. So the top line represents the furthest string away from the player, and the lowest line represents the closest string to the player as they look down at the uke. You read and play left to right.

There are more possible ways to play this song, in this key. 7 on the C-string can be played not only as 0 on the G-string, but *also* as 3 on the E-string. These overlaps are also very common on the guitar as well. Depending on your knowledge of the uke, as well as your desire to move your hands quickly and accurately, you can decide in the moment whether to switch strings or not (more advanced players tend to prefer switching strings whenever possible, as it limits hand movement - plus you can *combine* hand movement with string switching for extra speed). The extra spaces between notes signify "rests" (it's not nearly as exact as sheet music, but who cares? - you get the idea).

If these are both too hard for you to play - a better starting point would be to try this song (or something even simpler - like "Hot Cross Buns") on only one string. If you like to pluck with your index finger, you can play the song on the furthest string away from you (the A-string), and if you like to pluck with your thumb, we can play it on the closest string to you (the G-string). So, let's put tabs for all of these!

This is how you would play "Hot Cross Buns" on the closest string with your thumb:

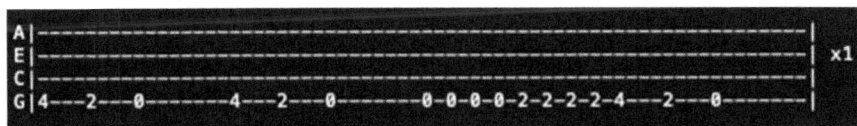

```
A |-------------------------------------------------------------|
E |-------------------------------------------------------------| x1
C |-------------------------------------------------------------|
G |4---2---0-------4---2---0-------0-0-0-0-2-2-2-2-4---2---0------|
```

5. Hot Cross Buns on the G-string

6. Hot Cross Buns on the G-string (Over the Shoulder)

...and this is how you would play "Hot Cross Buns" on the furthest string:

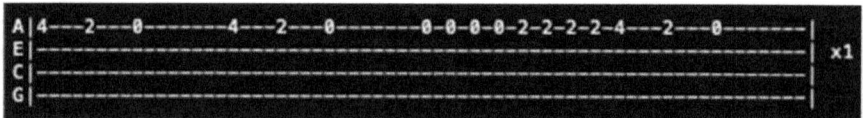

```
A|4---2---0---------4---2---0---------0-0-0-0-2-2-2-2-4---2---0-------|
E|------------------------------------------------------------------|  x1
C|------------------------------------------------------------------|
G|------------------------------------------------------------------|
```

7. Hot Cross Buns on the A-string

8. Hot Cross Buns on the A-string (Over the Shoulder)

Once you get this down - first of all, congrats! To increase the difficulty in these one-string versions of "Hot Cross Buns" - try playing the top tab with your *index* finger, and the bottom tab with your *thumb*. In other words, just try playing each tab with the opposite finger you had previously used. Or, try other fingers outside of those two! Once you've got those down, you can backtrack and try the earlier tabs for "Mary Had a Little Lamb."

These particular tabs represent single-note melodies, but you can use tabs to show how to play chords as well. Technically, any two notes played at once is a chord, but chords are typically played as triads. We'll touch more on this later, but here's a quick primer on chords. Triads are three note chords that represent a scale by taking the root, third, and fifth notes of the scale (and repeating these notes). For instance, a C major scale goes as follows - CDEFGABC. So a C major triad is made of the notes C, E, and G. On the ukulele, we play this chord with a C, E, G, and another C (most chords that don't have fancy extensions, on any stringed instrument, just use *and repeat* the notes from the triad). It's also one of the easiest chords to play on the guitar and looks like this in tab form:

```
A | 3- |
E | 0- |
C | 0- |
G | 0- |
```

🔊))

9. C Major Chord

Notice that all the numbers are lined up vertically. This means you should strum all of the strings at the same time (likely with your thumb with a flick of your right wrist). Since this particular chord features a "0" on the C, E, and G strings, you don't need to press down on those. You only would need to press down on the third fret of the A string, which makes another C. Now let's learn how to read this same chord (and more) with chord charts!

How To Read Chord Charts

Just like tabs, chord charts rely on illustrations - only, both the strings and the frets are illustrated. Since the strings and frets of the ukulele run perpendicular to each other, the drawing ends up looking like a cross-hatch pattern. It's usually done in a way where the headstock of the guitar would be at the top of the chart, as if you're holding the ukulele upwards. That C-major chord tab from earlier would look like this:

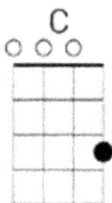

Notice the thicker line at the top, which is drawn that way to indicate the nut. The black circle on the furthest line to the right, sits on the third space between the horizontal lines, so it wants you to put a finger down on the third fret. It also is saying that you should strum all the strings without pressing anything on the other ones (hence the 0s at the top of the strings). Sometimes, you'll get even less information than that, though. This is what that looks like:

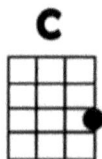

This means the exact same thing, but the lack of thick line at the top makes it a bit harder to parse. Once you've been playing for a while, this will be plenty of information for any new chord you learn (and you'll likely memorize the basic ones quite quickly). If possible, I like to flip these diagrams for people on their side, so that it looks like this:

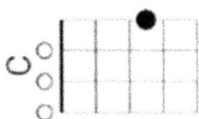

I like this because it actually looks like the ukulele as you look down on it (which many beginners will do); although this is a habit I picked up when teaching guitar, it obviously works for both instruments. However, I don't know if I've ever seen this in the wild, it might just be something I made up (the sideways chord chart). Or rather, it's probably just rare, and I haven't seen it in a long time. If the beginner student continues to struggle to read these charts, I'll draw a headstock coming out of the thick line that represents the nut, in order to help them visualize this.

Now that we know how to read these charts, let's learn a ton of chords!

Chapter 5

Basic Chords and Progressions

You can technically learn these chords, and their respective chord *shapes*, in any order you want. I could just put a giant list of all the diagrams here - and eventually, I *will*. But, certain chords tend to go better together, due to common patterns in music theory. Plus, some of these chords are easier to play than others. In fact, you might be able to get by while only able to play very few chords, and you can then supplement with the use of a capo. We'll explain what that is with a quick tangent later, but let's get into the basic chords.

If you turn on the radio in Hawaii, you will likely only hear songs with this chord progression: I - V - vi - IV. You don't need to know what that means in music theory jargon, but just know this - that results in these chords on the ukulele in easy mode (which is the best mode - ukulele is about having fun and kicking back!):

C Major:	A Minor	F major:	G Major:

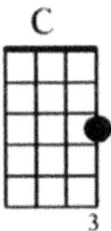   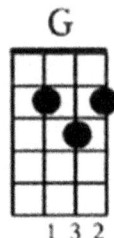

(The numbers underneath each diagram indicate which fingers they recommend you use to push down on the strings - 1 corresponds with your pointer, 2 with your middle finger, 3 with your middle finger, etc.) You'll be able to play countless songs just with these four chords. They're such a common set of chords, that multiple <u>meme songs </u>have been made about them. Plus, there's multiple incredibly common chord progressions *within* this set of four chords! Here are a few different ones you should be become acquainted with:

C major	G major	A minor	F major
C major	A minor	F major	G major
C major	F major	A minor	G major
A minor	F major	C major	G major

10. C-G-Am-F Whole Notes

11. C-Am-F-G Whole Notes

12. C-F-Am-G Whole Notes

13. Am-F-C-G Whole Notes

The top chord progression is *especially* common. It's actually the one we hear in perhaps the most famous ukulele song of all time ("Somewhere Over the Rainbow"). Although, sometimes G major will be swapped for E minor, for a bit more variety and interesting flavor. We can discuss *why* that makes for an interesting substitute later in the optional music theory section of this ebook, but for now - just know that E minor can be a more unique substitute for

G major. For that matter, D minor can be a more interesting substitute for F major. So, at this point, let's make sure we're on top of all of these chords:

C major, D minor, E minor, F major, G major, and A minor.

Two of those we haven't touched on yet. Let's get you some chord diagrams and picture demonstrations of those right quick:

D minor   E minor:

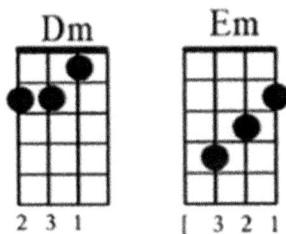

These chords are all "diatonic" for the key of C major - again, this is a music theory term we don't need to know yet - but basically, it means, they all conform to the scale. They're all in the C major scale - which has all white keys on a piano (no black keys), and every chord also only has white keys in it. But we'll come back to that later.

What if you only want to learn those chords, but someone wants you to play a song in a different key? Well, that's going to be doable thanks to the magic of the capo!

Quick Tangent - The Capo

The capo is a wonderful tool on any stringed instrument. It's most commonly used on the acoustic guitar, but you can get an edition for the ukulele as well. It holds down all of the strings on the same fret, bringing up the pitch of each string equally. Let's say you wanted to play this chord progression:

D major   A major   B minor   G major

This happens to be the typical I-V-vi-IV progression we've covered already, but this time, it's in the key of *D* major. So far, the only chord you know of that bunch is G major. BUT - every chord is exactly one whole-step above the chord progression we already learned!

C major + one whole-step = D major

G major + one whole-step = A major

A minor + one whole-step = B minor

F major + one whole-step = G major

So, since each fret is one half-step (and two frets = a whole-step) - you can use the same chord shapes you used earlier, and simply fasten the capo onto the second fret! This (of course) goes for other keys, as well. You can also use a capo made for guitars on a ukulele, although it might feel a bit big and unwieldy to play with. However, I only own a guitar capo, and I don't consider it *too* hard to play with on a ukulele (plus, you can't use a ukulele capo on a guitar, since it's too small - but you can use a guitar capo on a ukulele, so if you decide you'd like to play both instruments, you should maybe still get a guitar capo first). You can see a video of me playing this progression below:

🔊))

14. D-A-Bm-G using Capo

...and I'll be honest - the guitar capo *did* feel a bit in the way. And, since it's a bit too big for the instrument, you can actually twist it off the intended fret with your chord shape hand (i.e. your left hand). You can see that happen in this video, and how the high "C" (actually a D, thanks to the capo) gets out of tune at the end as a result:

🔊))

15. D-A-Bm-G using Capo Twist

You're probably better off spending $6-10 getting a capo actually made for the ukulele (or $15-20 for a nicer one) - plus, they just look so cute!

When I last visited Hawaii, my sister drove me around and we listened to the radio. Every song played on the radio used some variation of these chord progressions listed - it might be transposed into a different key than "C," but it all centered around those four chords. And, again, sometimes the F Major will be swapped out for a D minor, or the G major will be swapped out for an E minor. Or, a chord progression will go from a G major to an E minor (or vice versa), to lengthen that section of a piece (same with D minor / F major). So, make sure you are also familiar with the above chord progressions but with the minor substitutions for F and G major.

Of course, you may want to play different chord progressions. Or, play in different keys without a capo. Whatever your plan is, you'll want to learn other chords besides the ones we've listed. So let's tackle more of them!

But let's clarify - every chord has multiple "voicings" (i.e. more than way to play them). Depending on where you're coming from and where you're going, different voicings may work better than the ones you're used to. But we'll focus on the most common (and basic) voicings here.

Chapter 6

Note Names (Optional)

Notice how we haven't played any single-note melodies yet on the ukulele? They're actually a bit easier to play physically than chords, yet we're now six chapters in, and I've yet to touch on it. That's because single-note melodies are less conventionally played on the ukulele and a bit more complicated to understand than basic chord progressions (and you need to move your fingers relatively quickly, although you don't need to make as intricate of shapes with your fingers). More often than not - ukulele players will strum chords with their hands, and sing melodies with their voice. But - you still can play melodies, so we may as well understand note names and scales (more on the latter in the next chapter).

We need to recognize (and preferably memorize) the layout of the keys on a piano in order to understand note names. The black keys fit in between the white keys, and come in groups of two and three repeating. Perhaps instead of explaining it with text, here's a picture:

Again, as you can see - there's two black keys, then a break, then three, then two, then three, and that repeats up the keyboard. The white keys get plain note lettered note names - like A, B, C, etc. But the black keys get fancy names like "B-flat" and "F-sharp." More on that later - first, let's figure out which note is which on this keyboard.

As you can see, the C - our most important note, arguably - is the white key just to the left of the two black keys. F is just to the left of the three black keys. Notes go "up" from left to right, getting higher in pitch, and getting later in the alphabet (and the notes reset after G, after which they return to A).

In order to get to the black keys, you need to go up or down a half-step from a normally-named note. Start from any note - to get a black key that's a half-step above your starting note, you add the word "sharp" to it (which is labeled with the ♯ symbol). To go the opposite direction, you add the word "flat" to it (labeled with the ♭). To make things easier to type, ♯ can be replaced with a simple # or hashtag, and the ♭symbol can be typed with a simple lower-case "b." Anyway, let's label these black keys.

As you can see, each black key actually has *two* names. For instance, the lowest black key in this picture can be called C♯ or

Db. You can either "flatten" a D, and push it down a half-step, or you can "sharpen" a C to bring it up a half-step - either way, you'll end up on that key.

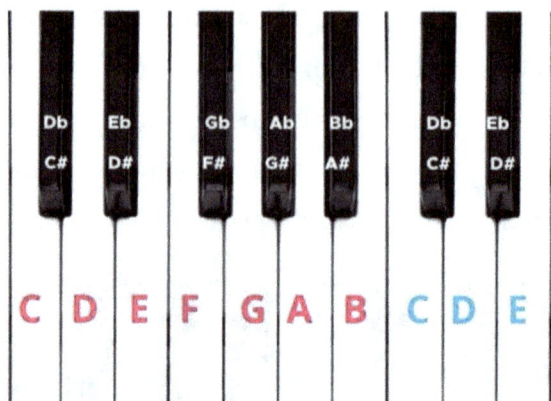

Why mention all of this stuff? Well, if you'd like to play single note melodies, it might help to know what note you're playing at any given time. And notice how most of the time, each letter is a whole step (or two half-steps) above the previous letter. For instance, D is two piano keys above C, or two half-steps. But this isn't always true! Notice how F is only a half-step above E, and C is only one half-step above B! That means that F is only one *fret* above E (and C is only one fret above B).

Now that we know what these different pitches look like on a piano keyboard, let's see what the notes on a ukulele look like! Of course, as always - this only applies to standard tuning. Still, here's the pitch of every fret on this standard ukulele (which is way more thorough than anyone could possibly need):

A	A#	B	C	C#	D	D#	E	F	F#	G	G#	A
E	F	F#	G	G#	A	A#	B	C	C#	D	D#	E
C	C#	D	D#	E	F	F#	G	G#	A	A#	B	C
G	G#	A	A#	B	C	C#	D	D#	E	F	F#	G

(etc.)

For the sake of simplicity, I labeled every "black key" as a sharp, and never used flats. Notice how there is no "sharp" note in between any of the Bs and Cs, or Es and Fs (just tying back into what we discussed earlier). And now that we know what all the pitches look like on a *ukulele* (as **well** as a piano), we can wrap our heads around how scales work. But that's another optional chapter, which will come later. Perhaps more urgently, we need to figure out how rhythm works on the ukulele, don't we?! Let's do it!

Chapter 7

Basic Rhythms and Strumming Patterns

Even though I'd like to avoid getting too in-depth on sheet music, notation, music theory, etc. unless it's absolutely necessary, I feel we should at least touch on basic rhythm notation. But just the basics, I promise!

Typically in western music, we notate 'notes' that follow the 'beat' with "quarter notes." By "the beat," I mean the general pulse of a given piece of music. When you listen to a song, you'll probably want to tap your toe or bob your head as you listen. The speed that most people would want to move their body to a given piece of music is notated with these quarter notes. They look like this: ♩

Most music is in a time signature called 4/4 (meaning 4 notes per 'measure'). When you see a drummer count in a song, they'll click their sticks 4 times, and yell "one, two, three, four!" and then everyone joins in. Drum beats generally restart after those four beats, and chunks of music (or "phrases") tend to come in groups of four of these "measures." There's lots of symmetry in music, and groupings of 4. There are alternate "time signatures," but we'll mostly focus on 4/4 (you can research these more unique and experimental rhythms after this book!).

Let's say you want to play notes that are twice as fast as the pulse of a song. Those would be called "eighth notes," and are notated as such: ♫. There are also slower notes than the pulse, which we typically think of as notes that are "held." These include "half notes" (which last for two beats), "whole notes" (which last for four beats), "dotted half notes" (which last for three beats), "dotted quarter notes" (which last for 1.5 beats), and many more different rhythms. But we'll mostly focus on quarter notes and eighth notes, as they make up most of the common strumming patterns.

We need to understand two more quick concepts - rests, and ties. Rests correspond to the rhythms above - e.g. There are quarter rests and eighth rests, just like half rests and whole rests. But we'll focus on the first two.

Quarter rests look like: 𝄽 and eighth rests look like this: 𝄾

But we can likely avoid needing rests if we use ties, which look like this: ⌣

Ties connect notes and make them last for their combined length of time. For instance - quarter notes are one beat apiece. If you tie two of them together, you'd hold *that* note for the length of *two* beats. Granted, you'll not see that rhythm very much, since half notes already mean "hold for two beats." But ties help musicians visualize more complicated rhythms, based on the addition of simpler rhythms.

Now we've got all the basics we need for rhythms! Except for *one* last concept - "*swung*" eighth notes.

When "swinging" eighth notes, the notes off of the beat are a bit late. If we count quarter notes as "One, Two, Three, Four," we'd count eighth notes as "One-and-two-and-three-and-four-and." When swinging rhythms, we play (or count) the "ands" just a bit late. Lots of ukulele music uses this style. Sometimes it's just easier to listen to swung patterns in actual music than analyzing like this - when you hear it, it's easier to *feel* it (and play it).

We'll need to get this feel down when covering the most common strumming pattern in both ukulele and acoustic guitar. We'll also need to understand quarter notes, eighth notes, and ties. That's why we covered all of the above - and to get that pattern down, we'll build it up piece by piece.

First, let's strum quarter notes. We'll use a C major chord for this entire section - as it's an easy chord, it's in the main key of the ukulele, and many, *many* uke songs are in the key of C major. Here's a recording of me strumming a C major chord as quarter notes at 110ish bpm:

16. C Major Quarter Notes

That would be notated as such:

Now let's add some eighth notes. In fact, let's turn the whole measure into eighth notes! Next, let's swing those eighth notes. If that's confusing for you, we'll start by comparing "straight" (normal eighth notes) with "swung" eighth notes. Here are couple recordings to help you hear the difference:

🔊

17. C Major 8th Notes (Straight)

18. C Major 8th Notes (Swung)

Either way, it looks like this in sheet music notation:

Now let's mix some quarter and eighth notes together. We'll leave beats 1 and 4 as quarter notes, and turn beats 2 and 3 into eighth notes. Make sure to try both straight and swung versions of this rhythm. That will sound and look like this:

🔊

19. C Major Q eeeeQ (Straight)

20. C Major Q eeeeQ (Swung)

Okay, time for the last step in this common strumming pattern! You've probably heard this pattern all over. In order to get this last pattern, we're going to add a tie that connects these eighth notes - the "and of 2," and the eighth note on beat 3. Alternatively, you can just put an eighth rest on beat 3 - the effect is the same, since the ukulele is a fairly percussive (or short-lasting) instrument. Notation-wise, that would look like this:

Here are videos of this strumming pattern, both swung and straight.

21. C Major Straight (Strumming Pattern 1)

22. C Major Swung (Strumming Pattern 1)

Notice the tie - it's a bit small, so it's hard to spot. Here's a quick label just to help point it out:

You've heard that strumming pattern before, right? You may not realize it, but you most likely have. We can also add eighth notes at the end on beat 4, replacing the last quarter note. Here's how that would look and sound, both in straight and swung rhythms:

You can try one of endless other strumming patterns, and there's a good chance you can figure them out by ear without notation. But it's generally easiest to play *any* strumming pattern like this: all of the "downbeats" (1, 2, 3, or 4) are strummed in a downward motion, and all of the "upbeats" (or, the "ands") are strummed in an upward motion. It doesn't matter if you have multiple downbeats in a row or upbeats - this makes strumming the easiest it can be. You end up just doing a constant up-and-down motion, and only hit the strings when you want to strum them. It's easy! If that's confusing, don't overthink it.

Let's try all of these strumming patterns - or at least the last few ones - with one of our tried and true chord progressions, the I-V-vi-IV (although you can try this with any of the other common, four-chord progressions listed earlier). The I-V-vi-IV one would go as such:

C major   >G major   >A minor   >F major

Try playing each chord for one measure, and change chords when the chord symbols above the rhythms change. That will look like this:

...and it will be sound like this (both "straight" and "swung" versions are attached):

25. C-G-Am-F Straight (Strumming Pattern 2)

26. C-G-Am-F Swung (Strumming Pattern 2)

Notice how, when a chord is major, there's no need to add any extra letters or symbols to it to designate what type of chord it is. If it's a *minor* chord, we can add a lowercase "m" or a "-" symbol afterward. Chords with fancy extensions - like 7ths - need extra characters to designate the type of chord they want you to play. More on that later!

But first, let's talk about another style of chord - not in terms of music theory, but in terms of how it's *played*. These are called "barre chords" (or, alternately, "bar chords").

Chapter 8

Barre Chords

If you're familiar with the concept of Barre Chords from playing the guitar, you can probably skip this section. If not, and you're new to any stringed instrument, we'll cover it quickly here!

Simply put, a barre chord is made when your fingers make a simple chord, and your pointer finger pushes down behind the chord shape on all the strings. Basically, you'll use your pointer finger like a human-operated, portable capo. Maybe this concept is difficult to grasp through text - so let's come up with an example.

Our C major chord was arguably the simplest chord we've learned so far. It only requires one finger, pressing down on the 3rd fret of the furthest (or "top") string. To refresh ourselves, this looks like so:

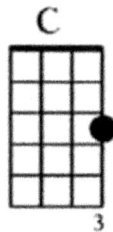

This gives us the notes, G, C, E, and C (the G, C, and E strings are all open, and the A string is played by pushing down on the 3rd fret - this raises what would be an A three half-steps, up to C). Just to refresh on that concept, here's a piano keyboard showing that C is, indeed, three half-steps above A:

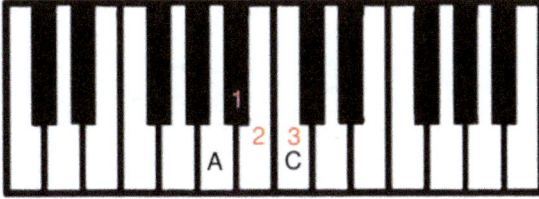

What if we wanted to play a Db major chord? This constitutes of a Db, F, and an Ab. Every note in this chord is exactly one half-step above the notes in a C major chord. There are multiple ways to play this chord (or "voicings"), but perhaps the most straightforward would be a barre chord.

In order to replicate a C major chord, but raise it a half-step: put your ring or pinky finger down on the *4th* fret of the A string. Then, press down on all the strings with your pointer finger on the first fret, making a "bar" that pushes down across the neck. That will end up looking like this from your point of view:

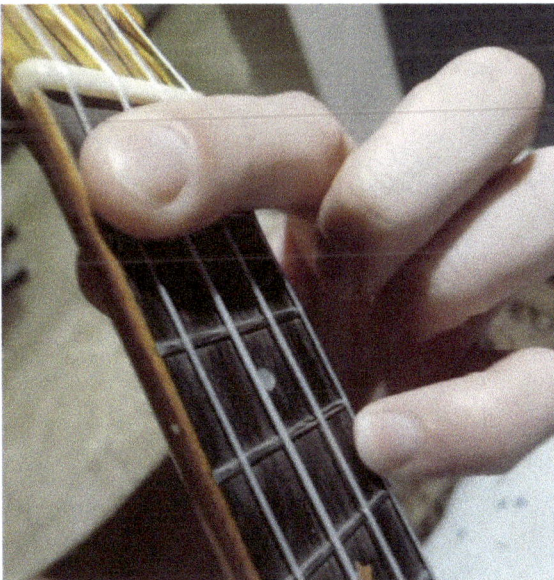

The chord diagram will end up looking like one of these:

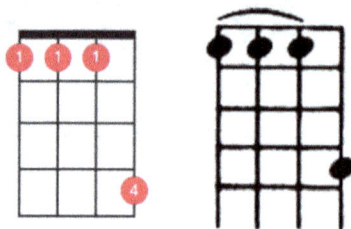

Notice how, on the first diagram, it tells you to press down on the first fret with your pointer finger (or the "1" finger) across all of those strings. The second diagram actually illustrates this "barre" shape with a tie-like symbol. You are meant to press down on all of the strings on the first fret. Since you pluck and/or strum strings on the *right* side of all of these frets, it doesn't matter if you push down in extra spots on the strings outside of the notes you're actually supposed to hear (as long as the extra fret finger placements happen to the *left* of the notes we want to hear). This makes barre chords work on any stringed instrument.

This means that you can also play a D major chord this same way (by putting a "barre" on the second fret, and pressing down on the 5th fret on the A string). Or, you can play an E♭ chord by repeating the process with a barre on the 3rd fret, and by playing the A string on the 6th fret, etc. And this is just one of many shapes that you can make a barre chord with.

Here's the same barre shape on the 3rd fret, making an E♭ major chord:

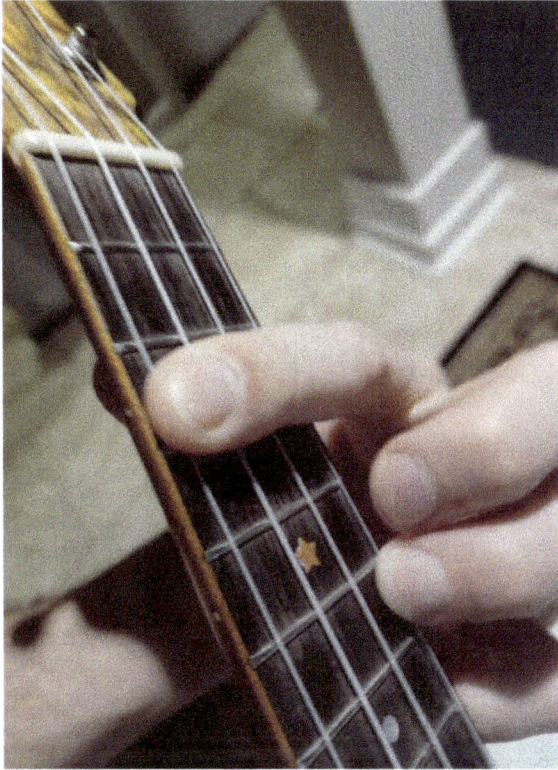

...and here is a vid of both those two barre chords - one anchored on the first fret, and one on the third fret:

🔊))

27. Barre Chords on Frets 1 and 3

Ukulele has way more options for barre chords than guitar does, since there are more simple chords available that leave your pointer finger free to make the "barre." This is because we only have four strings, instead of the six on the guitar. So, we can easily make barre chord "shapes" off all of these chords: C major, C major 7, C dominant 7, F major, A minor, A minor 7, G major 7 (which is sort of a "double barre" chord, if you will), D minor, and….you know what, it's a lot. It's not worth listing them all. Basically, if you can play a chord easily (especially with only one or two fingers in your left hand), and you can play it with your pointer finger free, and you have the dexterity to push down on all the strings with your pointer finger - then congrats, you can play just about any chord, thanks to barre chords!

Guitar is limited to far less barre chords, due to its 6 strings - generally, you're limited to A major, A minor, E major, E minor, and dominant 7 versions of those shapes with which to build your barre chords. There are other possible shapes, too, but after a while, they become more trouble than they're worth (if the shape itself is somewhat complex, and you have to add a barre to that, it's just easier to learn other voicings for said chords). Barre chords are still immensely useful on guitar, though - and learning them on ukulele makes for a great stepping stone to the guitar version of the same technique!

Chapter 9

Scales and Basic Music Theory (Optional)

As the title of this chapter indicates, this is somewhat optional information to play the ukulele; as mentioned earlier, most ukulele playing just consists of chord strumming anyways (and even melodies can be learned through tabs instead of sheet music). That said, understanding of scales and music theory certainly helps our understanding of the relationships of these chords, anyway.

The most common "keys" that songs can be based in are major and minor keys. If a song is in a major key, it will use the major scale, and songs in a minor key will use a minor scale. Most of the time, they'll use a "natural minor" scale, but there are also "melodic minor" and "harmonic minor scales." There's even "diminished" and "augmented" scales, but those are weird enough that we'll rarely see those.

Scales are used as the basis for our chords. The C-major scale is made up of all the white keys, so it's the easiest place to start. Let's examine how the C-major scale is formed; this way we can understand how all major scales are formed.

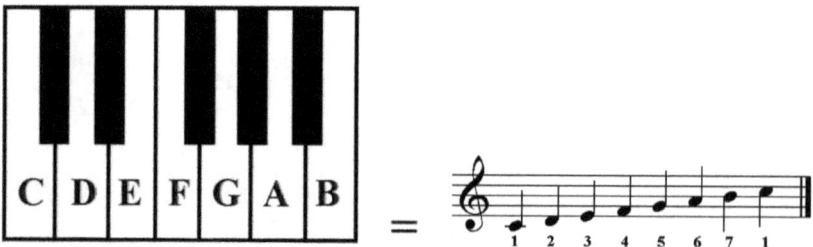

Now let's examine the scale steps of this major scale. Since the smallest gap between two keys on a keyboard is a "half-step," and a jump the size of two half-steps is known as a "whole-step," we can analyze each step of the scale as a half or a whole. In this diagram, I've labeled whole steps as "W" and half steps as "H."

This pattern of "WWHWWWH" forms every major scale. Take D-major, for example:

Minor scales can be made with the pattern "WHWWHWW," but they can also be made out of major scales in two different ways.

One way is by playing the major scale exactly the same but starting on the sixth step; for example, playing a C-major scale starting on "A."

This makes an A-minor scale, and since they share the same scale, A-minor is known as the "relative minor" of C-major (just as C-major is the relative major of A-minor).

A-Minor Scale

Another possible way to form a minor scale from a major scale is by lowering the 3rd, 6th, and 7th of a major scale by a half step. If we start with a C-major scale, this process leaves us with a C-minor scale, and since they share the same name, they are known as "parallel" major and minor keys from each other. Notice how after putting flats on the E, A, and B in the C-major scale, we get the "WHWWHWW" required for a minor scale. This can also be tested against the A-minor above.

Now that we have fully reviewed major and minor scales, we can use them to understand how chords are made. Let's briefly review that. The most common type of chord is a "triad" - those are made by playing the 1st, 3rd, and 5th notes of a scale at the same time. So our C major triad consists of a C, an E, and G, as you can see here:

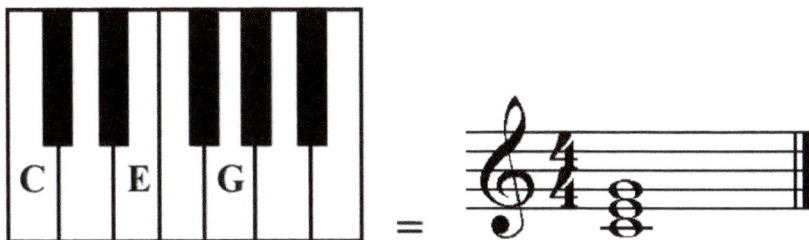

We can also use our knowledge of these major and minor scales to understand how to play melodic lines on the ukulele, if we'd like to. You can even combine these melodies with chords strummed at regular intervals, for what are called "chord melodies." Let's revisit which notes are which on our ukulele by checking out that picture with all of the note names on the neck and fretboard:

Now, our "home" key is in the key of C major (in standard tuning, of course). It's the easiest to play on ukulele *and* easiest to understand on *any* instrument. So, if we get rid of all of the "sharps," we'll end up with notes in our C major (or A minor) scale. For ease of located our "root" of C, I've enlarged and bolded the font for all C's:

We can use our knowledge of theory to understand how to play a major scale up the neck of the ukulele. First, check out how we would play our C major scale on the C string, without changing strings:

Notice how it's two frets from C to D (or a "whole step"), as it is from D to E, but only one fret from E to F. It follows the "WWHWWWH" pattern we mentioned earlier (where W = whole step, and H = half-step). Long term, playing up the neck like this isn't usually the best way to play scales - it's much easier for your hand to switch strings. This requires some knowledge of where the strings overlap, though, which can make it a bit tougher to get down at first. Here's how to play the same C major scale, while still starting on an open C-string and switching up the strings for minimal hand movement:

🔊

28. C Major Scales

You can also replace the G on the E string with an open G on the G-string - but that requires backtracking a string in the middle of a scale, then jumping *two* strings. This is awkward and unnatural for most - especially for those who started playing guitar before ukulele - so it might be easier to not do that. In order to play a minor scale, play any of these patterns, but start and end on A.

🔊

29. A Minor Scale

We'll gloss over that for a few reasons. For one, most ukulele songs aren't in a minor key - and, just to reiterate, you can definitely play the ukulele without playing any scales whatsoever. For instance, I play scales, do two-handed tapping, and make chord melodies every time I pick up a guitar, but find myself just strumming basic chords every time I pick up a ukulele. It just feels more natural!

In order to bypass some of this knowledge, but still learn chords in an efficient way - sometimes chord charts will be organized into "families" (aka groups of chords that tend to go together, as they make common chord progressions in the same key). Finding resources that describe these "families" might also be in your best interest! But, at the end of the day, knowing as many chords as possible, and being able to smoothly transition between *any* chords, will be the best long-term strategy for learning songs (as well as getting good with your barre chords, of course).

Chapter 10

Different Types of 7th Chords
(and when to use them) - (Semi-Optional)

So far, we've talked about normal triads - in other words, three note chords, based on the root, 3rd, and 5th of a scale. That also means that the root and the 3rd are a "third" away from each other, and the 3rd and the 5th are also a "third" away from each other (this "third" is the label for the distance - or "interval" - separating them, and we don't necessarily need to explain it now). If we add another "third" on top of the chord, we can get the "7th" of the scale, and add it to our chord for extra flavor. This will make a four-note chord.

As the title of this chapter suggests, you don't necessarily need to understand the music theory behind any of this. But, we might as well cover all the ins and outs of 7th chords, since you'll be playing them soon, anyway. They really aren't *too* complicated to understand (in terms of how they work, the different types, and when to use them).

So far, we've mostly dabbled with "**Major**" and "**Minor**" triads. Both of them feature a root, and a "Perfect 5th" (which happens to be 7 half-steps above the root - again, this is information you don't necessarily need to know, yet). The difference between these chords happens in the 3rd (the "Major" chord features a "3rd" that's *four* half-steps *above* the *root*, and only *three* half-steps *below* the *5th* - for the "Minor chord, these intervals are swapped).

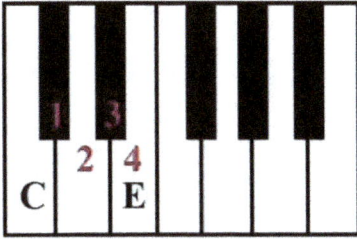
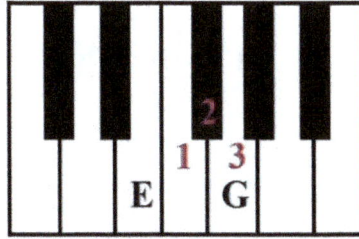

MAJOR THIRD   **MINOR THIRD**

(These are the two "thirds" in a major triad - the first interval is a "major third," and the second one is a "minor third").

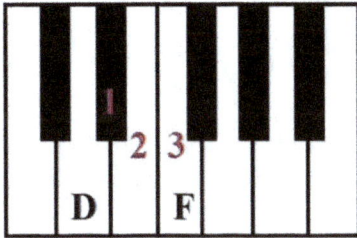

MINOR THIRD   **MAJOR THIRD**

Again, maybe this is all unnecessary information. Either way, we call the 3rd in a Major chord a "Major 3rd" (go figure), and we call it a "Minor 3rd" in a Minor chord (again, go figure). "Diminished" and "Augmented" triads use a different fifth than the major and minor chords - the diminished triad features two "minor 3rds" stacked on top of each other, so the "5th" ends up lower than its usual place of 7 half-steps above the root. In an augmented chord, the two intervals are major thirds stacked on top of each other, so the "5th" ends up higher than its usual place of 7 half-steps above the root. This looks like so, in the case of the augmented chord:

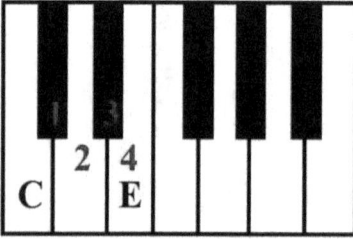

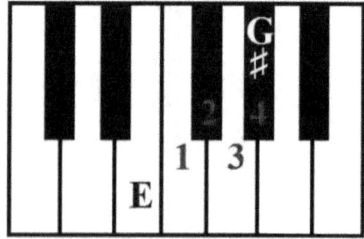

MAJOR THIRD   **MAJOR THIRD**

...and it looks like *this* in the case of the diminished chord:

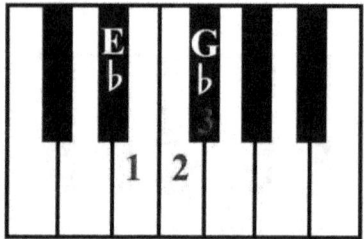

MINOR THIRD   **MINOR THIRD**

The reason we're covering all of this, is that these concepts will help us understand 7th chords. Major chords feature a major third, and a normal (perfect) 5th. Minor chords feature the minor third, and a normal (perfect) 5th. But what about 7ths?

Let's start with the "Major 7" chord. This one involves our major 3rd, and also the *7th note of the major scale* that bears the chord's name. You can also find this chord tone by going up a major 3rd (or, four half steps) from the perfect 5th. So, in the case of C, the C major chord tones are C, E, G, and B. That looks like this:

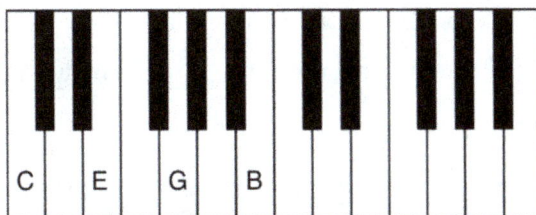

These are the first, third, fifth, and seventh notes of the C major scale. The "3rd" intervals up the chord are stacked as a major 3rd (four half-steps from C to E), a minor third (three half-steps from E to G), and a major 3rd (four half-steps from G to B). If we wanted to turn that into a "Minor 7" chord, we'd flatten the E (our "3rd") *and* the B (our "7th"). That would look like this:

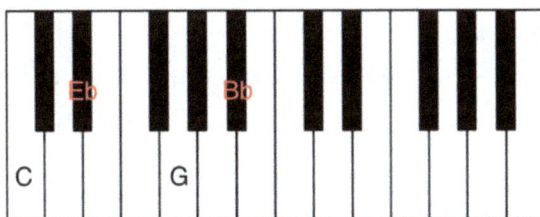

The gap between the root and the 3rd is a minor 3rd (only three half-steps from C to Eb), the gab from this minor third to the 5th is a major 3rd (four half-steps from Eb to G), and the gap from the 5th to the 7th is another minor 3rd (three half-steps from G to Bb). The next chord is a great one - it's fairly common, because it's very useful. It's called the "Dominant 7" chord.

The "Dominant 7 Chord" features a major triad, but a flattened 7th on top of it. By itself, it sounds "bluesy," but it's just as welcome in classical, pop, and all other mainstream contexts, as well. We'll get to why that is later, but first let's just describe a C-Dominant 7 right now. It's got a C, E, and G making up the primary triad, but a Bb up top. So it's got a major third on bottom, a minor third after that, and then it's capped off with *another* minor third. It looks like so:

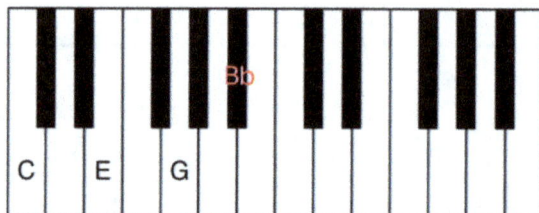

What if we were to keep the minor triad (with an Eb, if we're in the key of C), but add a B-natural up top? Aka, a major 7th? Well, this one's so weird and unusual, it doesn't even get a cute name. It's just a "Minor-Major-7," and it sounds weird. It's not diatonic to any key, and it's odd-ness makes it very rarely usable. So, here's an illustration of that chord. You probably won't see it anytime soon (although, by Murphy's Law, maybe it'll pop up in all of your favorite songs, who knows):

As we mentioned earlier, most of these 7th chords show up in popular music quite often. That's because, they're actually all regularly found diatonically - in other words, they make sense within a given scale of a song. Here are some common examples within our key and scale of C Major.

First, we've got the major 7 chord. This happens diatonically on our "One" chord (C major), as well as our "Four" chord (F major). We've already demonstrated the C major 7 on a piano keyboard, but here's a refresher:

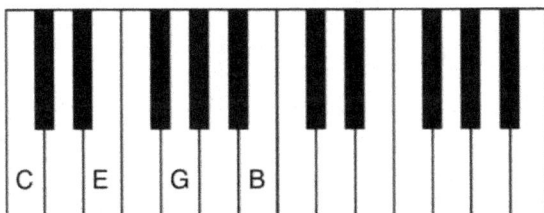

...and here's what the F-major 7 looks like on a piano keyboard:

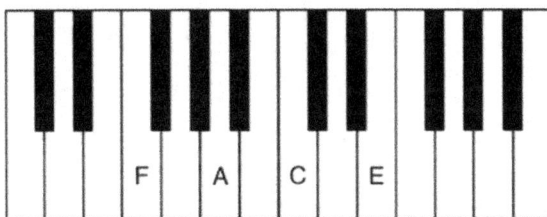

Diatonic "Minor 7" chords land on the "Two," "Three," and "Six" Chords. So in C Major, that ends up being D Minor 7, E Minor 7, and A Minor 7. They would look like so:

The last type of diatonic 7 chord would be a "half-diminished" - in other words, a diminished triad with a minor 7th. A fully-diminished 7 chord would feature just minor thirds between all the chord tones - so the 7 in a fully diminished chord isn't just minor, it's essentially flattened all the way down to the 6th. We're glossing over this here, because it's not super important. The point is, on the diatonic chord based on the 7th note of a major scale, you get a half-diminished chord (sometimes it's also called a "Minor-7, Flat-5," since that's another way to get to the same set of notes. That looks like this on the piano keyboard:

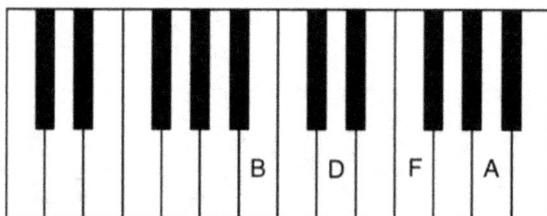

Obviously, any of these chords can be used on the black keys as well, but I'm using all-white-keys versions of these chords so that you can see diatonic versions in the key of C major (since that is both the easiest key to wrap our heads around *and* the easiest to play on a ukulele). And just a reminder - "diatonic" just means "chords that fit in the scale," essentially.

So, for a major scale, the diatonic seventh chords are as follows:

I maj 7

ii min 7

iii min 7

IV maj 7

V dom 7   (also notated as just V7)

vi min 7

vii min 7 b5   (also known as half-dim 7)

Notice we use lower-case letters for the Roman numerals on the minor and diminished chords. For a minor scale, we'd just start the same pattern where vi *used* to be. So that would look like this - and it would apply to our A *Minor* scale, which happens to *also* be all white keys:

i min 7

ii min 7 b5

III Maj 7

iv min 7

v min 7 *(often a major third on this chord is 'grandfathered' in, as it sounds epic)

VI Maj 7

VII dom 7 *This turns the V chord into a V7, or V dom 7 when adding a diatonic 7th

You didn't necessarily need to learn this. That's why this section was listed as optional, and why, despite the wordiness, it was also somewhat of a crash course. But the how and why of music theory can help explain patterns that will keep coming up as you play. For instance, if you're playing in the key of C, you're likely to see C major 7s, F major 7s, and G dominant 7s. It's also why you'd be likely to see a C *dominant* 7 before an F chord of some sort (C is the 'V' of F, so the Bb that gets introduced in the C dom 7 transitions nicely into an F major chord). You can see an example of this voice leading through 7th chords here:

🔊

30. Noodling with 7th Chords

The more of these patterns you pick up, the quicker you'll understand how music is made! That said, if you just get proficient moving to and from basically *any* chord, you can play the ukulele! So, all that's left is to learn as many chords as possible!

Chapter 11

Full Chord Chart

The following two pages are full of chords - there's well over 100 of them, and some of them have multiple voicings listed (alternate voicings are listed with white fingerings). Even with 100+ chords to work from, you can always find more chords to play (*and* more ways to play them). It's not an exhaustive list, but remembering the basic concepts of music theory - plus the notes on the fretboard - can give you access to unlimited chords and voicings. Happy playing!

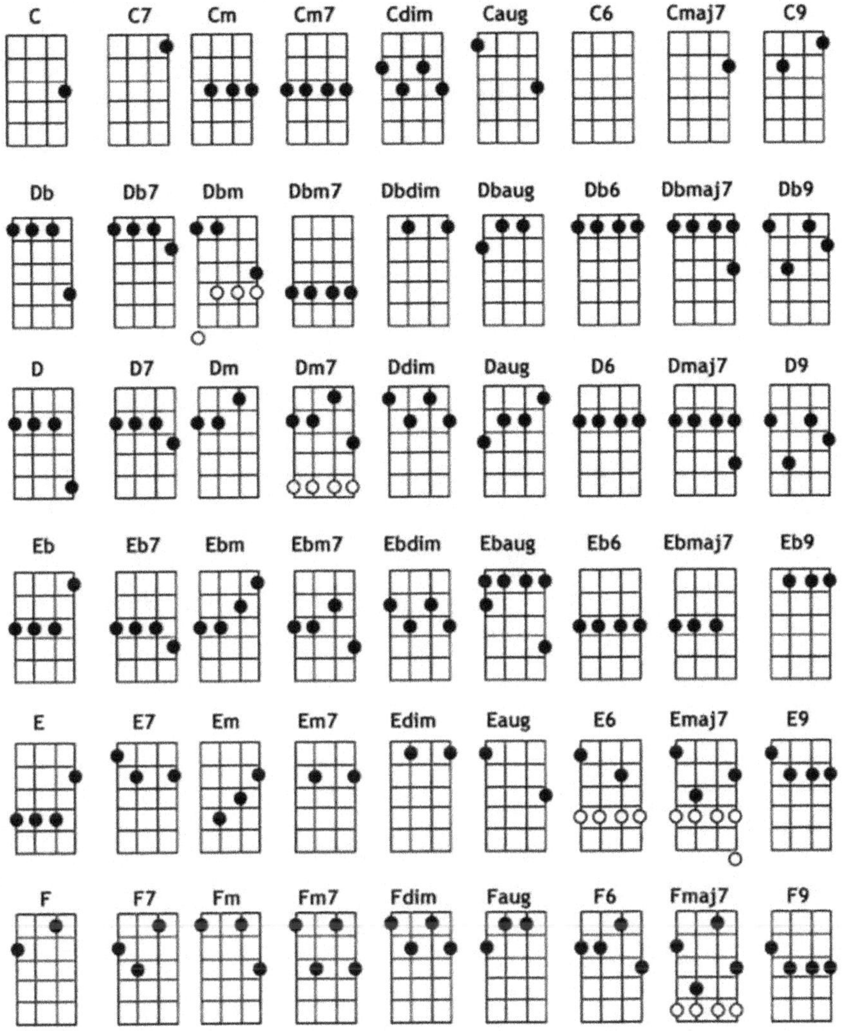
C C7 Cm Cm7 Cdim Caug C6 Cmaj7 C9
Db Db7 Dbm Dbm7 Dbdim Dbaug Db6 Dbmaj7 Db9
D D7 Dm Dm7 Ddim Daug D6 Dmaj7 D9
Eb Eb7 Ebm Ebm7 Ebdim Ebaug Eb6 Ebmaj7 Eb9
E E7 Em Em7 Edim Eaug E6 Emaj7 E9
F F7 Fm Fm7 Fdim Faug F6 Fmaj7 F9

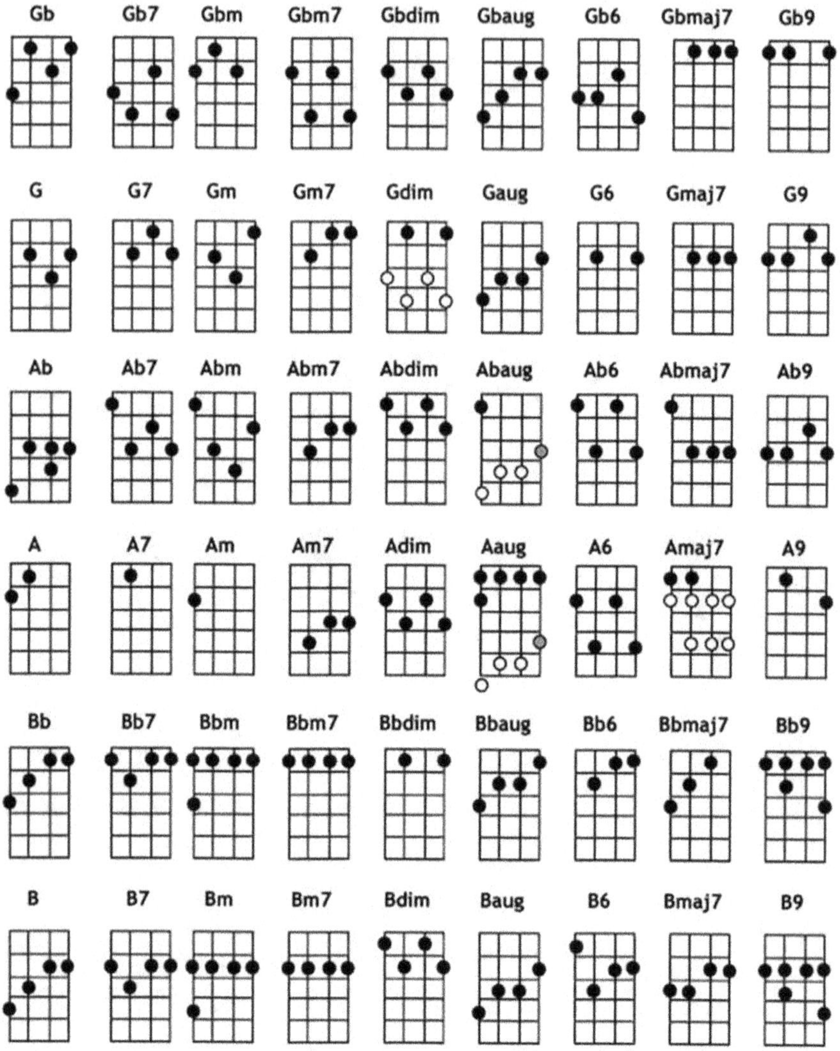
Gb
Gb7
Gbm
Gbm7
Gbdim
Gbaug
Gb6
Gbmaj7
Gb9
G
G7
Gm
Gm7
Gdim
Gaug
G6
Gmaj7
G9
Ab
Ab7
Abm
Abm7
Abdim
Abaug
Ab6
Abmaj7
Ab9
A
A7
Am
Am7
Adim
Aaug
A6
Amaj7
A9
Bb
Bb7
Bbm
Bbm7
Bbdim
Bbaug
Bb6
Bbmaj7
Bb9
B
B7
Bm
Bm7
Bdim
Baug
B6
Bmaj7
B9

Unlock Your Musical Potential:
Get 30% Off the Next Step in Your Instrumental Journey

As a token of appreciation for your dedication, we're excited to offer you an exclusive 30% discount on your next product when you sign up below with your email address.

Visit the link below:
https://bit.ly/40NikR2

OR

Use the QR Code:

Unlocking your musical potential is easier with ongoing guidance and support. Join our community of passionate musicians to elevate your skills and stay updated with the latest tips and tricks.

By signing up, you'll also receive our periodic newsletter with additional insights and resources to enhance your musical journey.

Your privacy is important to us. We won't spam you, and you can unsubscribe anytime.

Don't miss out on this opportunity to continue your musical journey with this special discount. Sign up now, and let's embark on this musical adventure together! 𝄞

www.ingramcontent.com/pod-product-compliance
Lightning Source LLC
LaVergne TN
LVHW022325080426
835508LV00013BA/1330